Holy Cross Mission - A Franciscan Community

A member of the Orthodox Anglican Church & The Orthodox Anglican Society of St. Francis

Pax et Bonum

Msgr. Dr.Anthony P. Giunta, PhD, ASF
1/20/2012

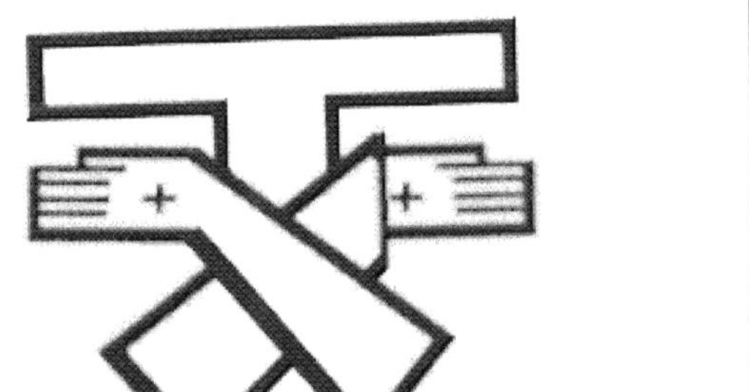

The Daily Offices as Prayed by the Brothers and Sisters of the Orthodox Anglican Society of St. Francis.

Morning Prayer

Prayer Before Office

Open my mouth, Lord, that I may bless your holy Name; cleanse also my heart from all vain, evil, and wandering thoughts; enlighten my understanding; inflame my affections; that I may say this Office worthily, with attention and devotion, and so be meet to be heard in the presence of your divine Majesty. Through Christ our Lord. Amen.

Opening Versicle with the Glory Be

It is customary to trace the Sign of the Cross with the thumb on the lips at the beginning of the Versicle. The "alleluia" may be added except during Lent and Holy Week.

All stand

Officiant O Lord, open thou our lips.
People And our mouth shall show forth thy praise.

Officiant and People

Glory to the Father, and to the Son, and to the Holy Spirit: as
it was in the beginning, is now, and will be for ever. Amen.

Except in Lent, Alleluia may be added.

The Antiphon to the Invitatory Psalm

The Antiphon is said at the beginning and the end of the Invitatory Psalm.

In Advent
Our King and Savior draweth nigh: O come, let us adore him.

On the Twelve Days of Christmas
Alleluia. Unto us a child is born: O come, let us adore him. Alleluia.

From the Epiphany through the Baptism of Christ, and on the Feasts of the Transfiguration and Holy Cross
The Lord hath manifested forth his glory: O come, let us adore him.

In Lent
The Lord is full of compassion and mercy: O come, let us adore him.

From Easter Day until the Ascension
Alleluia. The Lord is risen indeed: O come, let us adore him. Alleluia.

From Ascension Day until the Day of Pentecost
Alleluia. Christ the Lord ascendeth into heaven: O come, let us adore him. Alleluia.

On the Day of Pentecost
Alleluia. The Spirit of the Lord filleth the world: O come, let us adore him. Alleluia.

On Trinity Sunday
Father, Son, and Holy Ghost, one God: O come, let us adore him.

On other Sundays and Weekdays
The earth is the Lord's for he made it: O come, let us adore him.
or this
Worship the Lord in the beauty of holiness: O come, let us adore him.
or this
The mercy of the Lord is everlasting: O come, let us adore him.

The Alleluias in the following Antiphons are used only in Easter Season.

On Feasts of the Incarnation
[Alleluia.] The Word was made flesh and dwelt among us: O come, let us adore him. [Alleluia.]

On All Saints and other Major Saints' Days
[Alleluia.] The Lord is glorious in his saints: O come, let us adore him. [Alleluia.]

<u>*The Invitatory Psalm, The Venite*</u>

Psalm 95 may be used for the Invitatory. This would be especially suitable for Fridays, except during the fifty days of Easter. It is also appropriate during Lent and Holy Week, and at other penitential occasions.

<u>*Venite Psalm 95:1-7; 96:9,13*</u>

*O come, let us sing unto the Lord; **
let us heartily rejoice in the strength of our salvation.
*Let us come before his presence with thanksgiving, **
and show ourselves glad in him with psalms.

*For the Lord is a great God, **
and a great King above all gods.
*In his hand are all the corners of the earth, **
and the strength of the hills is his also.
*The sea is his and he made it, **
and his hands prepared the dry land.
*O come, let us worship and fall down **
and kneel before the Lord our Maker.
*For he is the Lord our God, **
and we are the people of his pasture
and the sheep of his hand.

*O worship the Lord in the beauty of holiness; **
let the whole earth stand in awe of him.
*For he cometh, for he cometh to judge the earth, **
and with righteousness to judge the world
and the peoples with his truth.

or Psalm 95

The Book of Common Prayer also permits the use of the "Jubilate Deo". In Easter Week and the fifty days of Easter, it is customary to use the "Christ our Passover" in place of the Invitatory.

Jubilate Deo Jubilate Psalm 100

*O be joyful in the Lord all ye lands; **
serve the Lord with gladness
and come before his presence with a song.

Be ye sure that the Lord he is God;
*it is he that hath made us and not we ourselves; **
we are his people and the sheep of his pasture.

O go your way into his gates with thanksgiving
and into his courts with praise; *
be thankful unto him and speak good of his Name.

For the Lord is gracious;
his mercy is everlasting; *
and his truth endureth from generation to generation.

Christ our Passover:

In Easter Week, in place of an Invitatory Psalm, the following is sung or said. It may also be used daily until the Day of Pentecost.

<u>Christ our Passover Pascha nostrum</u>
1 Corinthians 5:7-8; Romans 6:9-11; 1 Corinthians 15:20-22

Alleluia.

Christ our Passover is sacrificed for us, *
therefore let us keep the feast,
Not with old leaven,
neither with the leaven of malice and wickedness, *
but with the unleavened bread of sincerity and truth. Alleluia.

Christ being raised from the dead dieth no more; *
death hath no more dominion over him.
For in that he died, he died unto sin once; *
but in that he liveth, he liveth unto God.
Likewise reckon ye also yourselves to be dead indeed unto sin, *
but alive unto God through Jesus Christ our Lord. Alleluia.

Christ is risen from the dead, *
and become the first fruits of them that slept.
For since by man came death, *
by man came also the resurrection of the dead.
For as in Adam all die, *
even so in Christ shall all be made alive. Alleluia.

<u>The Psalms</u>
Consult the Ordo and the Calendar Tables of the Order, or the Daily Office Lectionary found

in The Book of Common Prayer, 1979, to obtain the proper Psalms. In the recitation of the Psalms, a pause is made at the asterisk "* ". The "Glory be to the Father" is said after each psalm or at the end of the selected psalms.

As an alternative to the above, the Psalms may be read on the thirty day cycle established in The Book of Common Prayer.

Old Testament Lesson

Consult the Ordo and the Calendar Tables of the Order, or the Daily Office Lectionary found in The Book of Common Prayer to obtain the proper Old Testament lesson.

The Old Testament Canticle

["A Song of Praise":
["A Song of Creation":
"A Song of Praise" is used except on Saturday for Morning Prayer, at which time "A Song of Creation" is used in its place.

Canticle 2 A Song of Praise Benedictus es, Domine Song of the Three Young Men, 29-34

Blessed art thou, O Lord God of our fathers; *
praised and exalted above all for ever.
Blessed art thou for the Name of thy Majesty; *
praised and exalted above all for ever.
Blessed art thou in the temple of thy holiness; *
praised and exalted above all for ever.
Blessed art thou that beholdest the depths,
and dwellest between the Cherubim; *
praised and exalted above all for ever.
Blessed art thou on the glorious throne of thy kingdom; *
praised and exalted above all for ever.
Blessed art thou in the firmament of heaven; *
praised and exalted above all for ever.
Blessed art thou, O Father, Son, and Holy Spirit; *
praised and exalted above all for ever.

Canticle 1 A Song of Creation Benedicite, omnia opera Domini

This Canticle may be shortened by omitting section II or III

I Invocation

*O all ye works of the Lord, bless ye the Lord; **
praise him and magnify him for ever.
*O ye angels of the Lord, bless ye the Lord; **
praise him and magnify him for ever.

II The Cosmic Order

*O ye heavens, bless ye the Lord; **
O ye waters that be above the firmament, bless ye the Lord;
*O all ye powers of the Lord, bless ye the Lord; **
praise him and magnify him for ever.

*O ye sun and moon, bless ye the Lord; **
O ye stars of heaven, bless ye the Lord;
*O ye showers and dew, bless ye the Lord; **
praise him and magnify him for ever.

*O ye winds of God, bless ye the Lord; **
O ye fire and heat, bless ye the Lord;
*O ye winter and summer, bless ye the Lord; **
praise him and magnify him for ever.

*O ye dews and frosts, bless ye the Lord; **
O ye frost and cold, bless ye the Lord;
*O ye ice and snow, bless ye the Lord; **
praise him and magnify him for ever.

*O ye nights and days, bless ye the Lord; **
O ye light and darkness, bless ye the Lord;
*O ye lightnings and clouds, bless ye the Lord; **
praise him and magnify him for ever.

III The Earth and its Creatures

*O let the earth bless the Lord; **
O ye mountains and hills, bless ye the Lord;
*O all ye green things upon the earth, bless ye the Lord; **
praise him and magnify him for ever.

O ye wells, bless ye the Lord; *
O ye seas and floods, bless ye the Lord;
O ye whales and all that move in the waters, bless ye the Lord; *
praise him and magnify him for ever.

O all ye fowls of the air, bless ye the Lord; *
O all ye beasts and cattle, bless ye the Lord;
O ye children of men, bless ye the Lord; *
praise him and magnify him for ever.

IV The People of God

O ye people of God, bless ye the Lord; *
O ye priests of the Lord, bless ye the Lord;
O ye servants of the Lord, bless ye the Lord; *
praise him and magnify him for ever.

O ye spirits and souls of the righteous, bless ye the Lord; *
O ye holy and humble men of heart, bless ye the Lord.
Let us bless the Father, the Son, and the Holy Spirit; *
praise him and magnify him for ever.

New Testament Lesson

Consult the Ordo and the Calendar Tables of the Order, or the Daily Office Lectionary found in The Book of Common Prayer to obtain the proper New Testament lesson.

The New Testament Canticle

The "Song of Zechariah" is used. It is customary to make the Sign of the Cross at the beginning of this Canticle. On Sundays the "We Praise Thee" [Te Deum Laudamus] is appropriate or the "Glory to God" [Gloria in excelsis].

Canticle 4 The Song of Zechariah Benedictus Dominus Deus Luke 1:68-79

Blessed be the Lord God of Israel, *
for he hath visited and redeemed his people;
And hath raised up a mighty salvation for us *
in the house of his servant David,
As he spake by the mouth of his holy prophets, *
which have been since the world began:
That we should be saved from our enemies, *

and from the hand of all that hate us;
To perform the mercy promised to our forefathers, *
and to remember his holy covenant;
To perform the oath which he sware to our forefather Abraham, *
that he would give us,
That we being delivered out of the hand of our enemies *
might serve him without fear,
In holiness and righteousness before him, *
all the days of our life.

And thou, child, shalt be called the prophet of the Highest, *
for thou shalt go before the face of the Lord
to prepare his ways;
To give knowledge of salvation unto his people *
for the remission of their sins,
Through the tender mercy of our God, *
whereby the dayspring from on high hath visited us;
To give light to them that sit in darkness
and in the shadow of death, *
and to guide our feet into the way of peace.

Glory to the Father, and to the Son, and to the Holy Spirit: *
as it was in the beginning, is now, and will be for ever. Amen.

We Praise Thee:

Canticle 7 We Praise Thee Te Deum laudamus

We praise thee, O God; we acknowledge thee to be the Lord.
All the earth doth worship thee, the Father everlasting.
To thee all Angels cry aloud,
the Heavens and all the Powers therein.
To thee Cherubim and Seraphim continually do cry:
Holy, holy, holy, Lord God of Sabaoth;
Heaven and earth are full of the majesty of thy glory.
The glorious company of the apostles praise thee.
The goodly fellowship of the prophets praise thee.
The noble army of martyrs praise thee.
The holy Church throughout all the world
doth acknowledge thee,

the Father, of an infinite majesty,
thine adorable, true, and only Son,
also the Holy Ghost the Comforter.

Thou art the King of glory, O Christ.
Thou art the everlasting Son of the Father.
When thou tookest upon thee to deliver man,
thou didst humble thyself to be born of a Virgin.
When thou hadst overcome the sharpness of death,
thou didst open the kingdom of heaven to all believers.
Thou sittest at the right hand of God, in the glory of the Father.
We believe that thou shalt come to be our judge.
We therefore pray thee, help thy servants,
whom thou hast redeemed with thy precious blood.
Make them to be numbered with thy saints,
in glory everlasting.

Glory to God:

Canticle 6 Glory be to God   Gloria in excelsis

Glory be to God on high,
and on earth peace, good will towards men.

We praise thee, we bless thee,
we worship thee,
we glorify thee,
we give thanks to thee for thy great glory,
O Lord God, heavenly King, God the Father Almighty.

O Lord, the only-begotten Son, Jesus Christ;
O Lord God, Lamb of God, Son of the Father,
that takest away the sins of the world,
have mercy upon us.
Thou that takest away the sins of the world,
receive our prayer.
Thou that sittest at the right hand of God the Father,
have mercy upon us.

For thou only art holy,
thou only art the Lord,

thou only, O Christ,
with the Holy Ghost,
art most high in the glory of God the Father. Amen.

Several other Canticles are provided from which you may select. However, the "Song of Simeon" and the "Song of Mary" are not used at Morning prayer.

The Apostles Creed

The Apostles' Creed

Officiant and People together, all standing

I believe in God, the Father almighty,
maker of heaven and earth;
And in Jesus Christ his only Son our Lord;
who was conceived by the Holy Ghost,
born of the Virgin Mary,
suffered under Pontius Pilate,
was crucified, dead, and buried.
He descended into hell.
The third day he rose again from the dead.
He ascended into heaven,
and sitteth on the right hand of God the Father almighty.
From thence he shall come to judge the quick and the dead.
I believe in the Holy Ghost,
the holy catholic Church,
the communion of saints,
the forgiveness of sins,
the resurrection of the body,
and the life everlasting. Amen.

The Salutation and The Lord's Prayer

The people stand or kneel

Officiant The Lord be with you.
People And with thy spirit.
Officiant Let us pray.

Officiant and People

Our Father, who art in heaven,
hallowed be thy Name,
thy kingdom come,
thy will be done,
on earth as it is in heaven.
Give us this day our daily bread.
And forgive us our trespasses,
as we forgive those who trespass against us.
And lead us not into temptation,
but deliver us from evil.
For thine is the kingdom, and the power, and the glory,
for ever and ever. Amen.

The Hail Mary

Hail Mary, full of grace, the Lord is with thee,
Blessed art thou among women,
and blessed is the fruit of thy womb, Jesus.
Holy Mary, Mother of God, pray for us sinners,
now and at the hour of our death. Amen.

The Suffrages
You may use either group A or group B.

A

V. O Lord, show thy mercy upon us;
R. And grant us thy salvation.
V. Endue thy ministers with righteousness;
R. And make thy chosen people joyful.
V. Give peace, O Lord, in all the world;
R. For only in thee can we live in safety.
V. Lord, keep this nation under thy care;
R. And guide us in the way of justice and truth.
V. Let thy way be known upon earth;
R. Thy saving health among all nations.
V. Let not the needy, O Lord, be forgotten;
R. Nor the hope of the poor be taken away.
V. Create in us clean hearts, O God;
R. And sustain us with thy Holy Spirit.

B

V. O Lord, save thy people, and bless thine heritage;
R. Govern them and lift them up for ever.
V. Day by day we magnify thee;
R. And we worship thy Name ever, world without end.
V. Vouchsafe, O Lord, to keep us this day without sin;
R. O Lord, have mercy upon us, have mercy upon us.
V. O Lord, let thy mercy be upon us;
R. As our trust is in thee.
V. O Lord, in thee have I trusted;
R. Let me never be confounded.

The Collect for the Day
Refer to the Ordo and Calendar Tables of the Order for the proper Collect.

Fixed Collects
For Friday, Saturday, and Sunday

A Collect for Sundays
O God, who makest us glad with the weekly remembrance of the glorious resurrection of thy Son our Lord: Grant us this day such blessing through our worship of thee, that the days to come may be spent in thy favor; through the same Jesus Christ our Lord. Amen.

A Collect for Fridays
Almighty God, whose most dear Son went not up to joy but first he suffered pain, and entered not into glory before he
was crucified: Mercifully grant that we, walking in the way of the cross, may find it none other than the way of life and
peace; through the same thy Son Jesus Christ our Lord. Amen.

A Collect for Saturdays
Almighty God, who after the creation of the world didst rest from all thy works and sanctify a day of rest for all thy creatures: Grant that we, putting away all earthly anxieties, may be duly prepared for the service of thy sanctuary, and that our rest here upon earth may be a preparation for the eternal rest promised to thy people in heaven; through Jesus Christ our Lord. Amen.

The following Collects are also fixed:
The Collect for Peace

A Collect for Peace
O God, who art the author of peace and lover of concord, in knowledge of whom standeth our eternal life, whose service is perfect freedom: Defend us, thy humble servants, in all assaults of our enemies; that we, surely trusting in thy defense, may not fear the power of any adversaries; through the might of Jesus Christ our Lord. Amen.

The Collect for Grace

A Collect for Grace
O Lord, our heavenly Father, almighty and everlasting God, who hast safely brought us to the beginning of this day: Defend us in the same with thy mighty power; and grant that this day we fall into no sin, neither run into any kind of danger; but that we, being ordered by thy governance, may do always what is righteous in thy sight; through Jesus Christ our Lord. Amen.

Other Collects may also be included.

The Franciscan Collect
O God, who opened the eyes of our holy Father St. Francis to the vocation of service to you in this world; grant grace to the members of the Third Order, that we, being crucified with Christ, may show forth among men the radiance of his risen life, who with you and the Holy Spirit lives and reigns one God, world without end. Amen.

or this

O God, who has joined to the Franciscan Order of the Divine Compassion a Third Order dedicated to your service, grant, we ask, that being knit together in one fellowship we may glorify your holy Name after the example of blessed Francis and win others to your love; through Jesus Christ our Lord. Amen.

Prayers for the Order for Each Day of the Week
[When reciting the Daily Office use the Collect for the current day of the week from the following:]

Sunday

O Blessed and glorious Trinity, in whom alone is perfect love, bless, we pray, the Franciscan Order of the Divine Compassion; that in humility, love and joy they may serve and worship you and be worthy followers of your servants, Francis and Clare; who lives and reigns one God for ever and ever. Amen.

Monday

Bless, O Lord, the friars in these latter days; and grant that, serving in humility, love and joy, they may draw many souls to follow you, who was lifted up upon the Cross to be the Savior of sinners; who now lives and reigns, God, world without end. Amen.

Tuesday

O God, pour your abundant blessing on those who, after the pattern of St. Clare, have left all to follow you in a life of poverty, penance and devotion. Assist them with your grace that they may persevere in their vocation to the end. Give them such increase of numbers as is according to your will and grant that all their needs may be supplied to the glory of your Name and the extension of your kingdom. Through Jesus Christ our Lord. Amen.

Wednesday

O God, who by the example of blessed Francis our Father moves your people to love of simple things, grant that after his pattern we may hold lightly to the things of this world and lay up for ourselves treasure in heaven. Amen.

Thursday

O Lord Jesus Christ, who inspired blessed Clare to hold fast the privilege of poverty and, with the blessed sacrament, to put to flight the armies of the infidel; grant us so to be emptied of the vain pomp and glory of the world and filled with the joy of your Presence that the enemy of souls may find in us nothing that is his.Amen.

Friday

Almighty God, who has taught us that in the Name of Jesus Christ alone is salvation; mercifully grant that your faithful people, ever glorying in his Name, may make your salvation known to all the world. Amen.

Saturday

We ask you, Lord, mercifully to pour the abundance of your grace into our hearts as we commemorate the holy virgin Mary, Mother of God, and sanctify our bodies in chastity and our souls in humility and love. Amen.

Closing Versicle and Response

V. Let us bless the Lord.
R. Thanks be to God.

From Easter Day through the Day of Pentecost "Alleluia, alleluia" may be added to the preceding versicle and response.

Benediction
V. May the souls of the faithful departed through the mercy of God rest in peace.
R. And may light perpetual shine upon them. Amen.

or this

Those provided in The Book of Common Prayer:

The grace of our Lord Jesus Christ, and the love of God, and the fellowship of the Holy Ghost, be with us all evermore. Amen.2 Corinthians 13:14

May the God of hope fill us with all joy and peace in believing through the power of the Holy Spirit. Amen.
Romans 15:13

Glory to God whose power, working in us, can do infinitely more than we can ask or imagine: Glory to him from generation to generation in the Church, and in Christ Jesus for ever and ever. Amen. Ephesians 3:20,21

MidMorning Prayer

FODC Mid-Morning Prayer
Opening Versicle with the Glory Be
The Alleluia may be added except during Lent and Holy Week
Officiant: + O God, make speed to save us
People: O Lord, make haste to help us.
Officiant: Glory to the Father, and to the Son, and to the Holy Spirit:
People: As it was in the beginning, is now, and will be for ever. Amen.
The Psalms
As appointed using the monthly cycle or the following:
From Psalm 113
*Give praise, you servants of the Lord; **
praise the Name of the Lord.
*Let the Name of the Lord be blessed, **
from this time forth for evermore.

*From the rising of the sun to its going down **
let the Name of the Lord be praised.
*The Lord is high above all nations, **
and his glory above the heavens.
At the end of the Psalms is said:
Officiant: Glory to the Father, and to the Son, and to the Holy Spirit:
People: As it was in the beginning, is now, and will be for ever. Amen.

A reading
O God, you will keep in perfect peace those whose minds are fixed on you; for in returning and rest we shall be saved in quietness and trust shall be our strength. (Isaiah 26:3; 30:15)
R. Thanks be to God.
Blessed be the God and Father of our Lord Jesus Christ! By his great mercy we have been born anew to a living hope through the resurrection of Jesus Christ from the dead. 1 Peter 1:3
R. Thanks be to God.
Kyrie and Lord's Prayer
Officiant: Lord have mercy upon us
People: Christ have mercy upon us
Officiant: Lord have mercy upon us
Kneeling
Our Father, who art in heaven,
hallowed be thy Name,
thy kingdom come,
thy will be done,
on earth as it is in heaven.
Give us this day our daily bread.
And forgive us our trespasses,
as we forgive those
who trespass against us.
And lead us not into temptation,
but deliver us from evil.
For thine is the kingdom,
and the power, and the glory,
for ever and ever. Amen.

The Hail Mary
Officiant: Hail Mary, full of grace, the Lord is with thee, Blessed art thou among women, and blessed is the fruit of thy womb, Jesus.

People: Holy Mary, Mother of God, pray for us sinners, now and at the hour of our death. Amen.

Officiant Lord, hear our prayer;
People And let our cry come to you.
Officiant Let us pray.

Collect: Prayer for the World
O heavenly Father, who has filled the world with beauty: Open our eyes to behold your gracious hand in all your works; that, rejoicing in your whole creation, we may learn to serve you with gladness; for the sake of him through whom all things were made, your Son Jesus Christ our Lord. Amen.

Prayer to Fulfill God's Will
O great God of Glory, enlighten the darkness of my mind. And give me, Lord, a correct faith, a firm hope, a perfect love that I may carry out your holy and true commands. Amen.

Officiant Let us bless the Lord.
People Thanks be to God.
Officiant + May the souls of the faithful departed through the mercy of God rest in peace.
People And may light perpetual shine upon them.

Noonday Prayer

Opening Versicle with the Glory Be
[Page 103. It is customary to make the sign of the cross at the beginning of the Versicle. The Alleluia may be added except during Lent and Holy Week.]

V.+ O God, make speed to save us.
R. O Lord, make haste to help us.
Glory to the Father, and to the Son, and to the Holy Spirit: as it was in the beginning, is now, and will be for ever. Amen.

The Psalms
[Pages 103-105. One or more of the Psalms may be used. In the recitation of the Psalms, a pause is made at the asterisk "". The Glory be to the Father is said after each psalm or at the end of the selected psalms. The psalms to be used are]:*

Psalm 119 [Lucerna pedibus meis]

*Your word is a lantern to my feet *
and a light upon my path.*

*I have sworn and am determined *
to keep your righteous judgments.*

*I am deeply troubled; *
preserve my life, O Lord, according to your word.*

*Accept, O Lord, the willing tribute of my lips, *
and teach me your judgments.*

*My life is always in my hand, *
yet I do not forget your law.*

*The wicked have set a trap for me, *
but I have not strayed from your commandments.*

*Your decrees are my inheritance for ever; *
truly, they are the joy of my heart.*

*I have applied my heart to fulfill your statutes *
for ever and to the end.*

Psalm 121 [Levavi oculos]

*I lift up my eyes to the hills; *
from where is my help to come?*

*My help comes from the Lord, *
the maker of heaven and earth.*

*He will not let your foot be moved *
and he who watches over you will not fall asleep.*

*Behold, he who keeps watch over Israel *
shall neither slumber nor sleep;*

*The Lord himself watches over you; *
the Lord is your shade at your right hand,*

*So that the sun shall not strike you by day, *
nor the moon by night.*

*The Lord shall preserve you from all evil; *
it is he who shall keep you safe.*

*The Lord shall watch over your going out and your coming in, *
from this time forth for evermore.*

Psalm 126 [In convertendo]

*When the Lord restored the fortunes of Zion, *
then were we like those who dream.*

*Then was our mouth filled with laughter, *
and our tongue with shouts of joy.*

*Then they said among the nations, *
"The Lord has done great things for them."*

*The Lord has done great things for us, *
and we are glad indeed.*

*Restore our fortunes, O Lord, *
like the watercourses of the Negev.*

*Those who sowed with tears *
will reap with songs of joy.*

*Those who go out weeping, carrying the seed, *
will come again with joy, shouldering their sheaves.*

*[At the end of the Psalms is said]:
Glory to the Father, and to the Son, and to the Holy Spirit: *
as it was in the beginning, is now, and will be for ever. Amen.*

The Short Reading

The love of God has been poured into our hearts through the Holy Spirit that has been given to us. Romans 5:5

R. Thanks be to God.

or this

If anyone is in Christ he is a new creation; the old has passed away, behold the new has come. All this is from God, who through Christ reconciled us to himself and gave us the ministry of reconciliation. 2 Corinthians 5:17-18

R. Thanks be to God.

or this

From the rising of the sun to its setting my Name shall be great among the nations, and in every place incense shall be offered to my Name, and a pure offering; for my Name shall be great among the nations, says the Lord of Hosts. Malachi 1:11

R. Thanks be to God.

The Kyrie and Lord's Prayer
Lord, have mercy.
Christ have mercy.
Lord, have mercy.

Our Father, who art in heaven,
hallowed be thy Name,
thy kingdom come,
thy will be done,
on earth as it is in heaven.
Give us this day our daily bread.
And forgive us our trespasses,
as we forgive those who trespass against us.
And lead us not into temptation,
but deliver us from evil. Amen.

The Hail Mary
Hail Mary, full of grace, the Lord is with thee,
Blessed art thou among women,
and blessed is the fruit of thy womb, Jesus.

Holy Mary, Mother of God, pray for us sinners,
now and at the hour of our death. Amen.

The Suffrages

V. Lord, hear our prayer;
R. And let our cry come to you.
Let us pray.

The Collects
[Page 107. One or more of the following Collects is said.]
Heavenly Father, send your Holy Spirit into our hearts, to direct and rule us according to your will, to comfort us in all our afflictions, to defend us from all error, and to lead us into all truth; through Jesus Christ our Lord. Amen.

or this

Blessed Savior, at this hour you hung upon the cross, stretching out your loving arms: Grant that all the peoples of the earth may look to you and be saved; for your tender mercies' sake. Amen.

or this

Almighty Savior, who at noonday called your servant Saint Paul to be an apostle to the Gentiles: We pray you to illumine the world with the radiance of your glory, that all nations may come and worship you; for you live and reign for ever and ever. Amen.

or this

Lord Jesus Christ, you said to your apostles, "Peace I give to you; my own peace I leave with you:" Regard not our sins, but the faith of your Church, and give to us the peace and unity of that heavenly City, where with the Father and the Holy Spirit you live and reign, now and forever. Amen.

The Closing Versicle and Response

V. Let us bless the Lord.
R. Thanks be to God.

The Benediction
V. May the souls of the faithful departed through the mercy of God rest in peace.
R. And may light perpetual shine upon them. Amen.

MidAfternoon Prayer

FODC Mid-Afternoon Prayer

The Invitatory and Psalter

All stand.

Officiant: + O God, make speed to save us
People: O Lord, make haste to help us.
Officiant: Glory to the Father, and to the Son, and to the Holy Spirit:
People: As it was in the beginning, is now, and will be for ever. Amen.

The Psalms
As appointed using the monthly cycle or the following:
Psalm 15:
Lord, who may dwell in your tabernacle? *
who may abide upon your holy hill?
Whoever leads a blameless life and does what is right, *
who speaks the truth from his heart.
There is no guile upon his tongue;
he does no evil to his friend; *
he does not heap contempt upon his neighbor.
In his sight the wicked is rejected, *
but he honors those who fear the Lord.
He has sworn to do no wrong *
and does not take back his word.
He does not give his money in hope of gain, *
nor does he take a bribe against the innocent.
Whoever does these things *
shall never be overthrown.

Officiant: Glory to the Father, and to the Son, and to the Holy Spirit:
People: As it was in the beginning, is now, and will be for ever. Amen.

A Short Reading

It is not ourselves that we proclaim; we proclaim Christ Jesus as Lord, and ourselves as your servants, for Jesus' sake. For the same God who said "Out of darkness let light shine," has caused his light to shine within us, to give the light of revelation – the revelation of he glory of God in the face of Jesus Christ. 2 Corinthians 4:5-6
R. Thanks be to God.

Officiant: Lord have mercy upon us
People: Christ have mercy upon us
Officiant: Lord have mercy upon us

Kneeling

Our Father, who art in heaven,
hallowed be thy Name,
thy kingdom come,
thy will be done,
on earth as it is in heaven.
Give us this day our daily bread.
And forgive us our trespasses,
as we forgive those
who trespass against us.
And lead us not into temptation,
but deliver us from evil.
For thine is the kingdom,
and the power, and the glory,
for ever and ever. Amen.

The Hail Mary
Officiant: Hail Mary, full of grace, the Lord is with thee, Blessed art thou among women, and blessed is the fruit of thy womb, Jesus.
People: Holy Mary, Mother of God, pray for us sinners, now and at the hour of our death. Amen.

Collect
O Lord Jesus Christ, you became poor for our sake, that we might be made rich through your poverty: Guide and sanctify, we pray, those whom you call to follow you under the vows of poverty, chastity, and obedience, that by their prayer and service they may enrich your Church,

and by their life and worship may glorify your Name; for you reign with the Father and the Holy Spirit, one God now and forever. Amen.

Intercessions and Thanksgivings may be offered.

Officiant Let us bless the Lord.
People Thanks be to God.
Officiant + May the souls of the faithful departed through the mercy of God rest in peace.
People And may light perpetual shine upon them.

Evening Prayer

Opening Versicle with the Glory Be

It is customary to make the Sign of the Cross at the beginning of the Versicle. The "alleluia" may be added except during Lent and Holy Week.

Officiant O God, make speed to save us.
People O Lord, make haste to help us.

Officiant and People

Glory to the Father, and to the Son, and to the Holy Spirit: as
it was in the beginning, is now, and will be for ever. Amen.

Except in Lent, Alleluia may be added.

The Invitatory - Phos Hilaron

O gracious Light,
pure brightness of the everliving Father in heaven,
O Jesus Christ, holy and blessed!

Now as we come to the setting of the sun,
and our eyes behold the vesper light,
we sing thy praises, O God: Father, Son, and Holy Spirit.

Thou art worthy at all times to be praised by happy voices,
O Son of God, O Giver of life,
and to be glorified through all the worlds.

<u>The Psalms</u>
Consult the Ordo and the Calendar Tables of the Order, or the Daily Office Lectionary found in The Book of Common Prayer, 1979, to obtain the proper Psalms. In the recitation of the Psalms, a pause is made at the asterisk "* ". The "Glory be to the Father" is said after each psalm or at the end of the selected psalms.

As an alternative to the above, the Psalms may be read on the thirty day cycle established in The Book of Common Prayer.

<u>Old Testament Lesson</u>
Consult the Ordo and the Calendar Tables of the Order, or the Daily Office Lectionary found in The Book of Common Prayer to obtain the proper Old Testament lesson.

<u>The Old Testament Canticle</u>
It is customary to make the Sign of the Cross at the beginning of this Canticle.

<u>The Song of Mary</u> <u>Magnificat</u> Luke 1:46-55
My soul doth magnify the Lord, *
 and my spirit hath rejoiced in God my Savior.
For he hath regarded *
 the lowliness of his handmaiden.
For behold from henceforth *
 all generations shall call me blessed.
For he that is mighty hath magnified me, *
 and holy is his Name.
And his mercy is on them that fear him *
 throughout all generations.
He hath showed strength with his arm; *
 he hath scattered the proud in the imagination of their hearts.
He hath put down the mighty from their seat, *
 and hath exalted the humble and meek.
He hath filled the hungry with good things, *
 and the rich he hath sent empty away.
He remembering his mercy hath holpen his servant Israel, *
 as he promised to our forefathers,
 Abraham and his seed for ever.

Glory to the Father, and to the Son, and to the Holy Spirit: *
as it was in the beginning, is now, and will be for ever. Amen.

New Testament Lesson
Consult the Ordo and the Calendar Tables of the Order, or the Daily Office Lectionary found in The Book of Common Prayer to obtain the proper New Testament lesson.

The New Testament Canticle
The "Song of Simeon" is used. It is customary to make the Sign of the Cross at the beginning of this Canticle. If Compline will be said, The "Song of the Redeemed" may be used.

The Song of Simeon Nunc dimittis *Luke 2:29-32*
*Lord, now lettest thou thy servant depart in peace, **
according to thy word;
*For mine eyes have seen thy salvation, **
which thou hast prepared before the face of all people,
*To be a light to lighten the Gentiles, **
and to be the glory of thy people Israel.

*Glory to the Father, and to the Son, and to the Holy Spirit: **
as it was in the beginning, is now, and will be for ever. Amen.

Canticle 19 The Song of the Redeemed Magna et mirabilia *Revelation 15:3-4*

O ruler of the universe, Lord God,
*great deeds are they that you have done, **
surpassing human understanding.
*Your ways are ways of righteousness and truth, **
O King of all the ages.

Who can fail to do you homage, Lord,
*and sing the praises of your Name? **
for you only are the holy One.
*All nations will draw near and fall down before you, **
because your just and holy works have been revealed.

*Glory to the Father, and to the Son, and to the Holy Spirit: **
as it was in the beginning, is now, and will be for ever. Amen.

The Apostles Creed
Officiant and People together, all standing

I believe in God, the Father almighty,
maker of heaven and earth;
And in Jesus Christ his only Son our Lord;
who was conceived by the Holy Ghost,
born of the Virgin Mary,
suffered under Pontius Pilate,
was crucified, dead, and buried.
He descended into hell.
The third day he rose again from the dead.
He ascended into heaven,
and sitteth on the right hand of God the Father almighty.
From thence he shall come to judge the quick and the dead.
I believe in the Holy Ghost,
the holy catholic Church,
the communion of saints,
the forgiveness of sins,
the resurrection of the body,
and the life everlasting. Amen.

The Salutation and The Lord's Prayer
The people stand or kneel

Officiant The Lord be with you.
People And with thy spirit.
Officiant Let us pray.

Officiant and People

Our Father, who art in heaven,
hallowed be thy Name,
thy kingdom come,
thy will be done,
on earth as it is in heaven.
Give us this day our daily bread.
And forgive us our trespasses,
as we forgive those who trespass against us.
And lead us not into temptation,
but deliver us from evil.
For thine is the kingdom, and the power, and the glory,
for ever and ever. Amen.

The Hail Mary

Hail Mary, full of grace, the Lord is with thee,
Blessed art thou among women,
and blessed is the fruit of thy womb, Jesus.
Holy Mary, Mother of God, pray for us sinners,
now and at the hour of our death. Amen.

The Suffrages

You may use either group A or group B.

A

V. O Lord, show thy mercy upon us;
R. And grant us thy salvation.
V. Endue thy ministers with righteousness;
R. And make thy chosen people joyful.
V. Give peace, O Lord, in all the world;
R. For only in thee can we live in safety.
V. Lord, keep this nation under thy care;
R. And guide us in the way of justice and truth.
V. Let thy way be known upon earth;
R. Thy saving health among all nations.
V. Let not the needy, O Lord, be forgotten;
R. Nor the hope of the poor be taken away.
V. Create in us clean hearts, O God;
R. And sustain us with thy Holy Spirit.

B

That this evening may be holy, good, and peaceful,
We entreat thee, O Lord.

That thy holy angels may lead us in paths of peace and goodwill,
We entreat thee, O Lord.

That we may be pardoned and forgiven for our sins and offenses,
We entreat thee, O Lord.

That there may be peace to thy Church and to the whole world,
We entreat thee, O Lord.

That we may depart this life in thy faith and fear, and not be condemned before the great judgment seat of Christ,
We entreat thee, O Lord.

That we may be bound together by thy Holy Ghost in the communion of [_________ and] all thy saints, entrusting one another and all our life to Christ,
We entreat thee, O Lord.

The Collect of the Day
Refer to the Ordo and Calendar Tables of the Order for the proper Collect.

Fixed Collects
[For Friday, Saturday, and Sunday:

A Collect for Sundays
Lord God, whose Son our Savior Jesus Christ triumphed over the powers of death and prepared for us our place in the new Jerusalem: Grant that we, who have this day given thanks for his resurrection, may praise thee in that City of which he is the light; and where he liveth and reigneth for ever and ever. Amen.

A Collect for Fridays
O Lord Jesus Christ, who by thy death didst take away the sting of death: Grant unto us thy servants so to follow in faith where thou hast led the way, that we may at length fall asleep peacefully in thee, and awake up after thy likeness; for thy tender mercies' sake. Amen.

A Collect for Saturdays
O God, the source of eternal light: Shed forth thine unending day upon us who watch for thee, that our lips may praise thee, our lives may bless thee, and our worship on the morrow may give thee glory; through Jesus Christ our Lord. Amen.

The following Collects are also fixed:

The Collect for Peace:
O God, from whom all holy desires, all good counsels, and all just works do proceed: Give unto thy servants that peace which the world cannot give, that our hearts may be set to obey thy commandments, and also that by thee, we, being defended from the fear of all enemies, may pass our time in rest and quietness; through the merits of Jesus Christ our Savior. Amen.

The Collect for Aid against Perils:
Lighten our darkness, we beseech thee, O Lord; and by thy great mercy defend us from all perils and dangers of this night; for the love of thy only Son, our Savior Jesus Christ. Amen.

Other Collects may also be included.

The Franciscan Collects
O God, who opened the eyes of our holy Father St. Francis to the vocation of service to you in this world; grant grace to the members of the Third Order, that we, being crucified with Christ, may show forth among men the radiance of his risen life, who with you and the Holy Spirit lives and reigns one God, world without end. Amen.

or this

O God, who has joined to the Franciscan Order of the Divine Compassion a Third Order dedicated to your service, grant, we ask, that being knit together in one fellowship we may glorify your holy Name after the example of blessed Francis and win others to your love; through Jesus Christ our Lord. Amen.

Prayers for the Order for Each Day of the Week
[When reciting the Daily Office use the Collect for the current day of the week from the following:]

Sunday
O Blessed and glorious Trinity, in whom alone is perfect love, bless, we pray, the Franciscan Order of the Divine Compassion; that in humility, love and joy they may serve and worship you and be worthy followers of your servants, Francis and Clare; who lives and reigns one God for ever and ever. Amen.

Monday
Bless, O Lord, the friars in these latter days; and grant that, serving in humility, love and joy, they may draw many souls to follow you, who was lifted up upon the Cross to be the Savior of sinners; who now lives and reigns, God, world without end. Amen.

Tuesday
O God, pour your abundant blessing on those who, after the pattern of St. Clare, have left all to follow you in a life of poverty, penance and devotion. Assist them with your grace that they may persevere in their vocation to the end. Give them such increase of numbers as is according

to your will and grant that all their needs may be supplied to the glory of your Name and the extension of your kingdom. Through Jesus Christ our Lord. Amen.

Wednesday

O God, who by the example of blessed Francis our Father moves your people to love of simple things, grant that after his pattern we may hold lightly to the things of this world and lay up for ourselves treasure in heaven. Amen.

Thursday

O Lord Jesus Christ, who inspired blessed Clare to hold fast the privilege of poverty and, with the blessed sacrament, to put to flight the armies of the infidel; grant us so to be emptied of the vain pomp and glory of the world and filled with the joy of your Presence that the enemy of souls may find in us nothing that is his.Amen.

Friday

Almighty God, who has taught us that in the Name of Jesus Christ alone is salvation; mercifully grant that your faithful people, ever glorying in his Name, may make your salvation known to all the world. Amen.

Saturday

We ask you, Lord, mercifully to pour the abundance of your grace into our hearts as we commemorate the holy virgin Mary, Mother of God, and sanctify our bodies in chastity and our souls in humility and love. Amen.

Closing Versicle and Response

V. Let us bless the Lord.
R. Thanks be to God.

Benediction

V. May the souls of the faithful departed through the mercy of God rest in peace.
R. And may light perpetual shine upon them. Amen.

or this

Those provided in The Book of Common Prayer may also be used.

The grace of our Lord Jesus Christ, and the love of God, and the fellowship of the Holy Ghost, be with us all evermore. Amen.
2 Corinthians 13:14

May the God of hope fill us with all joy and peace in believing through the power of the Holy Spirit. Amen.
Romans 15:13

Glory to God whose power, working in us, can do infinitely more than we can ask or imagine: Glory to him from generation to generation in the Church, and in Christ Jesus for ever and ever. Amen.
Ephesians 3:20,21

Compline

The Officiant begins

The Lord Almighty grant us a peaceful night and a perfect end. Amen.

Opening Versicle and Response

V. + Our help is in the Name of the Lord;
R. The maker of heaven and earth.

The Confession

Let us confess our sins to God.

Almighty God, our heavenly Father: We have sinned against you, through our own fault, in thought, and word, and deed, and in what we have left undone. For the sake of your Son our Lord Jesus Christ, forgive us all our offenses; and grant that we may serve you in newness of life, to the glory of your Name. Amen.

Prayer For Forgiveness
May the Almighty God grant us forgiveness + of all our sins, and the grace and comfort of the Holy Spirit. Amen.

The Second Versicle and Response
[Page 128: It is customary to make the Sign of the Cross at the beginning of the Versicle]:

V. + O God, make speed to save us.
R. O Lord, make haste to help us.

Officiant and People

+ Glory to the Father, and to the Son, and to the Holy Spirit: as it was in the beginning, is now, and will be for ever. Amen.
[Except in Lent add]: Alleluia.

The Psalms

[One or more of the following At the end of the Psalms is sung or said "The Glory Be"]:

Psalm 4 [Cum invocarem]

*Answer me when I call, O God, defender of my cause; **
you set me free when I am hard-pressed;
have mercy on me and hear my prayer.

*"You mortals, how long will you dishonor my glory? **
how long will you worship dumb idols
and run after false gods?"

*Know that the Lord does wonders for the faithful; **
when I call upon the Lord, he will hear me.

*Tremble, then, and do not sin; **
speak to your heart in silence upon your bed.

*Offer the appointed sacrifices **
and put your trust in the Lord.

*Many are saying, "Oh, that we might see better times!" **
Lift up the light of your countenance upon us, O Lord.

*You have put gladness in my heart, **
more than when grain and wine and oil increase.

*I lie down in peace; at once I fall asleep; **
for only you, Lord, make me dwell in safety.

Psalm 31 [In te, Domine, speravi]

In you, O Lord, have I taken refuge;
*let me never be put to shame: **
deliver me in your righteousness.

*Incline your ear to me; **
make haste to deliver me.

Be my strong rock, a castle to keep me safe,
*for you are my crag and my stronghold; **
for the sake of your Name, lead me and guide me.

*Take me out of the net that they have secretly set for me, **
for you are my tower of strength.

*Into your hands I commend my spirit, **
for you have redeemed me,
O Lord, O God of truth.

<u>Psalm 91 [Qui habitat]</u>
*He who dwells in the shelter of the Most High **
abides under the shadow of the Almighty.

He shall say to the Lord,
*"You are my refuge and my stronghold, **
my God in whom I put my trust."

*He shall deliver you from the snare of the hunter **
and from the deadly pestilence.

He shall cover you with his pinions,
*and you shall find refuge under his wings; **
his faithfulness shall be a shield and buckler.

*You shall not be afraid of any terror by night, **
nor of the arrow that flies by day;

*Of the plague that stalks in the darkness, **
nor of the sickness that lays waste at mid-day.

A thousand shall fall at your side
*and ten thousand at your right hand, **
but it shall not come near you.

*Your eyes have only to behold **
to see the reward of the wicked.

*Because you have made the Lord your refuge, **
and the Most High your habitation,

*There shall no evil happen to you, **
neither shall any plague come near your dwelling.

*For he shall give his angels charge over you, **
to keep you in all your ways.

*They shall bear you in their hands, **
lest you dash your foot against a stone.

*You shall tread upon the lion and adder; **
you shall trample the young lion and the serpent under your feet.

Because he is bound to me in love,
*therefore will I deliver him; **
I will protect him, because he knows my Name.

*He shall call upon me, and I will answer him; **
I am with him in trouble;
I will rescue him and bring him to honor.

With long life will I satisfy him,
and show him my salvation.

Psalm 134 [Ecce nunc]
*Behold now, bless the Lord, all you servants of the Lord,**
you that stand by night in the house of the Lord.

*Lift up your hands in the holy place and bless the Lord; **
the Lord who made heaven and earth bless you out of Zion.

+ Glory to the Father, and to the Son, and to the Holy Spirit: as it was in the beginning, is now, and will be for ever. Amen.

The Scripture Passage

Lord, you are in the midst of us, and we are called by your Name: Do not forsake us, O Lord our God. Jeremiah 14:9,22

R. Thanks be to God.

or this

Come to me, all who labor and are heavy-laden, and I will give you rest. Take my yoke upon you, and learn from me; for I am gentle and lowly in heart, and you will find rest for your souls. For my yoke is easy, and my burden is light. Matthew 11:28-30

R. Thanks be to God.

or this

May the God of peace, who brought again from the dead our Lord Jesus, the great shepherd of the sheep, by the blood of the eternal covenant, equip you with everything good that you may do his will, working in you that which is pleasing in his sight; through Jesus Christ, to whom be glory for ever and ever. Hebrews 13:20-21

R. Thanks be to God.

or this

Be sober, be watchful. Your adversary the devil prowls around like a roaring lion, seeking someone to devour. Resist him, firm in your faith. 1 Peter 5:8-9a

R. Thanks be to God.

The Versicle and Responses

V. Into your hands, O Lord, I commend my spirit;
R. For you have redeemed me, O Lord, O God of truth.
V. Keep us O Lord, as the apple of your eye;
R. Hide us under the shadow of your wings.

The Kyrie and Lord's Prayer

Lord, have mercy.
Christ have mercy.

Lord, have mercy.

Our Father, who art in heaven, hallowed be thy Name, thy kingdom come, thy will be done, on earth as it is in heaven. Give us this day our daily bread. And forgive us our trespasses, as we forgive those who trespass against us. And lead us not into temptation, but deliver us from evil. Amen.

The Hail Mary

Hail Mary, full of grace, the Lord is with thee,
Blessed art thou among women,
and blessed is the fruit of thy womb, Jesus.
Holy Mary, Mother of God, pray for us sinners,
now and at the hour of our death. Amen.

The Versicle, Response and Collects

V. Lord, hear our prayer;
R. And let our cry come unto you.

Let us pray.

Be our light in the darkness, O Lord, and in your great mercy defend us from all perils and dangers of this night; for the love of your only Son, our Savior Jesus Christ. Amen.

or this

Be present, O merciful God, and protect us through the hours of this night, so that we who are wearied by the changes and chances of this life may rest in your eternal changelessness; through Jesus Christ our Lord. Amen.

or this

Look down, O Lord, from your heavenly throne, and illumine this night with your celestial brightness; that by night as by day your people may glorify your holy Name; through Jesus Christ our Lord. Amen.

or this

Visit this place, O Lord, and drive far from it all snares of the enemy; let your holy angels dwell with us to preserve us in peace; and let your blessing be upon us always; through Jesus Christ our Lord. Amen.

Collect for Saturday

We give you thanks, O God, for revealing your Son Jesus Christ to us by the light of his resurrection: Grant that as we sing your glory at the close of this day, our joy may abound in the morning as we celebrate the Paschal mystery; through Jesus Christ our Lord. Amen.

[One of the following additional prayers found on page 134 may be added].

Keep watch, dear Lord, with those who work, or watch, or weep this night, and give your angels charge over those who sleep. Tend the sick, Lord Christ; give rest to the weary, bless the dying, soothe the suffering, pity the afflicted, shield the joyous; and all for your love's sake. Amen.

or this

O God, your unfailing providence sustains the world we live in and the life we live; Watch over those, both night and day, who work while others sleep, and grant that we may never forget that our common life depends upon each others toil; through Jesus Christ our Lord. Amen.

Song of Simeon with Antiphon

Guide us waking, O Lord, and guard us sleeping; that awake we may watch with Christ, and asleep we may rest in peace.
[In Easter add; Alleluia, alleluia, alleluia]

Lord, you now have set your servant free
to go in peace as you have promised;

For these eyes of mine have seen the Savior,
whom you have prepared for all the world to see;

A Light to enlighten the nations,
and the glory of your people Israel.

+ Glory to the Father, and to the Son, and to the Holy Spirit;
as it was in the beginning, is now, and will be for ever. Amen.

Guide us waking, O Lord, and guard us sleeping; that awake we may watch with Christ, and asleep we may rest in peace.

The Versicle, Response and Benediction

V. Let us bless the Lord.
R. Thanks be to God.

Let us pray.

The almighty and merciful Lord, + Father, Son, and Holy Spirit, bless us and keep us. Amen.

The Marian Antiphon

Antiphon 1
[Said from Evening Prayer of the Saturday before 1 Sunday in Advent through Evening Prayer of Feb. 2]
Kindly Mother of our Redeemer, pray for us who, though fallen, strive to rise again. You, who brought forth, to all nature's wonder, nature's Lord, your own creator: Mother yet a virgin ever more, who at Gabriel's speaking received the Ave; towards us sinners show your pity.

[Said from Evening Prayer of the Saturday before the 1 Sunday in Advent through Morning Prayer of the Vigil of Christmas]
V. The Angel of the Lord brought tidings of Mary.
R. And she conceived by the Holy Spirit.

O Lord, pour your grace into our hearts: that, as we have known the incarnation of your Son Jesus Christ by the message of an Angel; so by his Cross and passion we may be brought to the glory of his resurrection. Through the same Christ our Lord. Amen.

[Said from Evening Prayer of the Vigil of Christmas through Evening Prayer on Feb. 2]
V. After Child-bearing you remained a pure Virgin.
R. Mother of God, intercede for us.

O God, who by the child-bearing of a pure Virgin has bestowed on all mankind the rewards of everlasting life: grant that we may know the succor of her intercession, through whom we have been found worthy to receive the Author of life, even Jesus Christ thy Son our Lord. Amen.

Antiphon II

[Said from Morning Prayer of Feb. 3 to Evening Prayer of Wednesday in Holy Week]
Hail, O Queen, on high enthroned,
Hail, O Lady, by Angels owned;
Jesse's rod; yea heaven's portal
Whence hath shone earth's Light immortal:
Hail, O Virgin, most renowned,
Hail, O truly worthy Maiden:
Pray Christ for us so burden-laden.

V. Accept my praise, O hallowed Virgin.
R. Pray that I may have strength against your enemies.

Lord, mercifully assist us in our infirmity: that like as we do now commemorate blessed Mary Ever-Virgin, Mother of God; so by the help of her prayers we may die to our former sins and rise again to newness of life. Through the same Christ our Lord. Amen.

Antiphon III

[Said from Evening Prayer of Holy Saturday through Morning Prayer of the Vigil of the Most Holy Trinity]
Rejoice, Queen Mother of heaven, alleluia;
Christ whom meetly thou bearest is risen, alleluia;

His forsaying thus fulfilling, alleluia:
Offer to God thy praying, alleluia.

V. Rejoice and be exceeding glad, O Virgin Mary, alleluia.
R. For the Lord is risen indeed, alleluia.

O God, who by the resurrection of your Son our Lord Jesus Christ has given joy to the world: grant that, through the prayers of his Mother, the Virgin Mary, we may obtain the joys of everlasting life. Through the same Christ our Lord. Amen.

Antiphon IV
[Said from Evening Prayer of the Vigil of the Most Holy Trinity through Morning Prayer of the Saturday before the 1 Sunday of Advent]
All hail, O holy Queen, Mother exceeding merciful; Life's spring, sweet comfort, our Hope-bearer, all hail. To thee our plaint we lift, children of Eve yet in exile. To thee our aspiring, and longing and weeping, lift we from this vale of sorrow. Ah then, Mary, be our intercessor; hither vouchsafe to turn thine eyes compassionate, and look upon us. And Jesus, blessed offspring of thy womb, O Mother, show thou to us when earthly exile endeth. O gentle, O loving, O gracious Virgin Mary.

V. Pray for us, O holy Mother of God.
R. That we may be worthy of the promises of Christ.

Almighty, everlasting God, who by the co-operation of the Holy Spirit prepared the body and soul of the glorious Virgin-Mother Mary to become a dwelling place meet for your son: grant that as we rejoice in her commemoration; so by her fervent intercession we may be delivered from present evils and from everlasting death. Through the same Christ our Lord. Amen.

The Morning Office

[The Morning and Evening Prayers which immediately follow herewith are not of obligation, but they do constitute the "Daily Office" appointed by the Minister-General to be read by the "Companions" (Associates) of the Order in the hope and expectation that they will wish to pattern their daily prayer life, as far as their individual circumstances will allow, after the prayer life expected of the Brothers and Sisters of Penitence. This "Daily Office" does not necessarily satisfy the Daily Office rule requirements of the Order's Brothers and Sisters, who must remain in compliance with the requirements of their individually approved Rule(s) of Life.]

MORNING PRAYER

The Sign of The Cross
By the sign of the cross deliver us from our enemies, you who are our God. + In the Name of the Father, and of the Son, and of the Holy Spirit. Amen.

The Opening Prayer
Open my mouth, Lord, that I may bless your holy Name; cleanse also my heart from all vain, evil, and wandering thoughts; enlighten my understanding; inflame my affections; that I may say this Office worthily, with attention and devotion, and so be meet to be heard in the presence of thy divine Majesty. Through Christ our Lord.Amen.

The Lord's Prayer
Our Father, who art in heaven, hallowed be thy Name, thy kingdom come, thy will be done, on earth as it is in heaven. Give us this day our daily bread. And forgive us our trespasses, as we forgive those who trespass against us. And lead us not into temptation, but deliver us from evil. Amen.

The Hail Mary
Hail Mary, full of grace, the Lord is with thee,
Blessed art thou among women,
and blessed is the fruit of thy womb, Jesus.
Holy Mary, Mother of God, pray for us sinners,
now and at the hour of our death. Amen.

V. O God, make speed to save us.

R. O Lord, make haste to help us.

The Glory Be

Glory be to the Father, and to the Son, and to the Holy Spirit.
As it was in the beginning, is now, and ever shall be, world without end. Amen.

The Psalms Appointed

[Here the Psalm(s) appointed for morning prayer are read: use either the Psalm(s) from the thirty day cycle corresponding to the day the Psalm is to be read, or use the Psalm(s) appointed as given in the Book of Common Prayer].

[Immediately before reading the Psalms(s) appointed as above, the following is said:]
Francis poor and lowly.

[Here recite the Psalms, then follows:]
Francis poor and lowly entereth heaven rich: and is honored with the songs of heaven. (Alleluia)

V. Blessed are the poor in spirit. [Alleluia]
R. For theirs is the Kingdom of Heaven. [Alleluia]

The Apostle's Creed

I believe in God, the Father almighty,
creator of heaven and earth.
I believe in Jesus Christ, his only Son, our Lord.
He was conceived by the power of the Holy Spirit
and born of the Virgin Mary.
He suffered under Pontius Pilate,
was crucified, died, and was buried.
He descended to the dead.
On the third day he rose again
He ascended into heaven,
and is seated at the right hand of the Father.
He will come again to judge the living and the dead.
I believe in the Holy Spirit,
the holy catholic Church,
the communion of saints,

the forgiveness of sins,
the resurrection of the body, +
and the life everlasting. Amen.

The Morning Offering
[The Franciscan Morning Prayer]
Jesus Lord, I offer you this new day because I believe in you, love you, hope all things in you and thank you for your blessings. I am sorry for having offended you and forgive everyone who has offended me. Lord, look on me and leave in me peace and courage and your humble wisdom that I may serve others with joy, and be pleasing to you all day.

The Prayer for Franciscans
Grant, O Lord, to your whole Church [and especially to the Franciscan Order of the Divine Compassion], many souls endued with the spirit and vision of Saint Francis: and call them together under the Holy Rule; that the work you once began in manifesting thy glory in the lowly may be continued in our generation. Through Christ our Lord. Amen.
V. O Lord hear my prayer.
R. And let my cry come unto thee.

Let us pray.

The Closing Prayer
[Written by St. Francis as a concluding prayer for "The Hours"]

V. "Let us bless our Lord and God, living and true; to him we must attribute all praise, glory, honor, blessing, and every good forever. Amen."

[And then follows:]
R. Thanks be to God.

V. May the souls of the faithful departed through the mercy of God rest in peace.
R. And may light perpetual shine upon them. Amen.

The Evening Office

[The Morning and Evening Prayers which immediately follow herewith are <u>not</u> of obligation, but they do constitute the "Daily Office' appointed by the Minister-General to be read by the 'Companions' (Associates) of the Order in the hope and expectation that they will wish to pattern their daily prayer life, as far as their individual circumstances will allow, after the prayer life expected of the Brothers and Sisters of Penitence. This "Daily Office" does <u>not</u> necessarily satisfy the Daily Office rule requirements of the Order's Brothers and Sisters, who must remain in compliance with the requirements of their individually approved Rule(s) of Life.]

EVENING PRAYER

The Sign of The Cross

+ In the Name of the Father, and of the Son, and of the Holy Spirit. Amen. Blessed be the holy and undivided Trinity now and forever.

The Opening Prayer

O Lord, in union with that divine intention with which you rendered your praises to God while on earth, I desire to offer this my Office of prayer to you. Amen.

The Lord's Prayer

Our Father, who art in heaven, hallowed be thy Name, thy kingdom come, thy will be done, on earth as it is in heaven. Give us this day our daily bread. And forgive us our trespasses, as we forgive those who trespass against us. And lead us not into temptation, but deliver us from evil. Amen.

The Hail Mary

Hail Mary, full of grace, the Lord is with thee,
Blessed art thou among women,
and blessed is the fruit of thy womb, Jesus.
Holy Mary, Mother of God, pray for us sinners,
now and at the hour of our death. Amen.

The Glory Be

Glory be to the Father, and to the Son, and to the Holy Spirit.
As it was in the beginning, is now, and ever shall be, world without end. Amen.

The Psalms Appointed

[Here the Psalm(s) appointed for evening prayer are read: use either the Psalm(s) from the thirty

day cycle corresponding to the day the Psalm is to be read, or use the Psalm(s) appointed as given in the Book of Common Prayer].

[Immediately before reading the Psalms(s) appointed as above, the following is said:]
Francis poor and lowly.

[Here recite the Psalms, then follows:]

Francis poor and lowly entereth heaven rich: and is honored with the songs of heaven. (Alleluia)

V. Blessed are the poor in spirit. [Alleluia]
R. For theirs is the Kingdom of Heaven. [Alleluia]

The Thanksgiving
How shall I be able to thank you, O Lord, for all your favors? You have thought of me from all eternity; you have brought me forth from nothing; you have given your life to redeem me, and you continue still, daily to pour your grace and blessing into my life. Alas, my God, what return can I make you for your benefits and in particular for the favors of this day. I praise you, I bless you. With all the Saints, especially St. Francis, St. Clare, St. Louis and St. Elizabeth, I praise you.

The Examination of Conscience
O Holy Spirit, eternal source of light, give me light to know the sins I have committed this day and grant me the grace to be truly sorry for them.

or this

O God, show me my sins. O God, make me sorry for my sins. O God, deliver me from my sins.

[Here follows a brief examination of conscience]

The Act of Contrition
O my God, I am heartily sorry for having sinned against you, who are all-good and deserving of all my love. I firmly resolve, with the help of your grace, to sin no more, and to avoid the occasions of sin.

The Confession of Sin
Most merciful God, we confess that we have sinned against you in thought, word, and deed, by

what we have done, and by what we have left undone. We have not loved you with our whole heart; we have not loved our neighbors as ourselves. We are truly sorry and we humbly repent. For the sake of your Son Jesus Christ, have mercy on us and forgive us; that we may delight in your will, and walk in your ways, to the glory of your Name. Amen.

or this

Almighty and most merciful Father,
we have erred and strayed from thy ways like lost sheep,
we have followed too much the devices and desires of our own hearts,
we have offended against thy holy laws,
we have left undone those things which we ought to have done,
and we have done those things which we ought not to have done,
But thou, O Lord, have mercy upon us,
spare thou those who confess their faults,
restore thou those who are penitent,
according to thy promises declared unto mankind
in Christ Jesus our Lord;
and grant, O most merciful Father, for his sake,
that we may hereafter live a godly, righteous, and sober life,
to the glory of thy Holy Name. Amen.

The Prayer for God's Forgiveness
+ Almighty God have mercy on us, forgive us all our sins through our Lord Jesus Christ, strengthen us is all goodness, and by the power of the Holy Spirit keep us in eternal life. Amen.

The Petition
Pour down your blessing, O Lord, on your whole church: on the Franciscan Order of the Divine Compassion, its Right Reverend Bishop Protector, its Minister-General, all those assisting him/them, and all the Brothers, Sisters, and Companions of the Order; on all Bishops and other clergy everywhere; on all the faithful; on this country; on our elected officials and all superiors, temporal and spiritual; on our parents, relatives, friends and enemies. Help the poor, the sick, and the dying; comfort the lonely and the abandoned.

Have mercy on this household and grant that humility, peace and charity may rule therein. Grant that we may love, fear, and serve thee faithfully all our days. Through our Lord and Savior Jesus Christ. Amen.

V. Vouchsafe, O Lord, this night to keep us without sin.
R. Have mercy on us, O Lord, have mercy on us.

The Night Blessing

Visit this place, O Lord, and drive far from it all snares of the enemy; let your holy angels dwell with us to preserve us in peace; and let your blessing be upon us always; through Jesus Christ our Lord. Amen.

The Closing Prayer

[Written by St. Francis as a concluding prayer for "The Hours"]

V. "Let us bless our Lord and God, living and true; to him we must attribute all praise, glory, honor, blessing, and every good forever. Amen."

[And then follows:]

R. Thanks be to God.

V. May the souls of the faithful departed through the mercy of God rest in peace.

R. And may light perpetual shine upon them. Amen.

www.ingramcontent.com/pod-product-compliance
Ingram Content Group UK Ltd.
Pitfield, Milton Keynes, MK11 3LW, UK
UKHW051134260726
13967UKWH00010B/3050